Anne Gagnon

with the participation of
Pierre Richard

Grammar EXPRESS

**Essentials
of English Grammar**

CEC

LES ÉDITIONS CEC INC.

8101, boul. Métropolitain Est, Anjou, Qc, Canada H1J 1J9
Téléphone: (514) 351-6010   Télécopieur: (514) 351-3534

Managing Director, ESL:
Leena M. Sandblom

Production Manager:
Danielle Latendresse

Project Editor:
Jaime M. Demperio

Pedagogical Consultant:
Lydia Lagloire

Cover and Page Design:
Dominique Gagnon

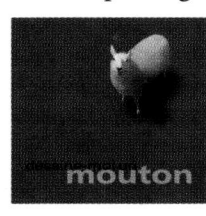

To the memory of my father,
Leo Gagnon

© 1999, Centre Éducatif et Culturel inc.
8101, boul. Métropolitain Est
Anjou, Québec H1J 1J9

This book is explicitly excluded from any photocopy agreements in existence.
Photocopying of any part of *Grammar Express* is illegal without prior written
permission from the publisher.

Dépôt légal, Bibliothèque nationale du Québec, 2e trimestre 1999
Legal deposit, National Library of Canada, 2nd quarter 1999

ISBN 2-7617-1567-5

Printed in Canada

1   2   3   4   5   6   03   02   01   00   99

Table of Contents

Parts of Speech

Nouns

Definition: A noun describes a person *(Michel)*, place *(Montreal)*, idea *(discovery)*, thing *(desk)*, animal *(dog)*, quality *(honesty)*, or action *(work)*. Nouns can be proper *(Boston/Mr. Jones)*, common *(cities/trout)*, abstract *(hatred/jealousy)*, concrete *(egg/trees)*, or collective *(football team/jury)*.

RULES FOR SPELLING PLURAL NOUNS

REGULAR SPELLINGS

Add **-s** to most countable nouns to form the plural.	*tree, tree**s**; individual, individual**s**; apple, apple**s***
Add **-es** when a singular noun ends in **-s, -z, -ch, -sh,** or **-x.**	*class, class**es**; couch, couch**es**; bush, bush**es**; tax, tax**es***
Add only **-s** when a final **-ch** ending sounds like /k/.	*stomach, stomach**s**; epoch, epoch**s**; monarch, monarch**s***

NOUNS ENDING IN -Y

When a noun ends in **-y** preceded by a consonant, change the **-y** to **-i** and add **-es.**	*lady, lad**ies**; library, librar**ies**; party, part**ies***
When a noun ends in **-y** preceded by a vowel, add only an **-s.**	*day, day**s**; tray, tray**s**; valley, valley**s***

NOUNS ENDING IN -F OR -FE

When a one-syllable noun ends in **-f** or **-fe**, change the **-fe** to **-ves.**	*knife, kni**ves**; life, li**ves**; self, sel**ves***
Exceptions: belief, belief**s**; chief, chief**s**; gulf, gulf**s**; roof, roof**s**; safe, saf**es**	

NOUNS ENDING IN -O

Usually when a noun ends in **-o** preceded by a consonant, add **-es.**	*hero, hero**es**; mosquito, mosquito**es**; potato, potato**es***
If a vowel precedes the **-o**, add only **-s.**	*radio, radio**s**; zoo, zoo**s***

IRREGULAR SPELLINGS

Some nouns have irregular plural spellings.	*child, children; foot, feet; goose, geese; (wo)man, (wo)men; mouse, mice; ox, oxen; tooth, teeth*
Some nouns have the same spelling in the singular and the plural.	*deer, fish, means, series, sheep*
Some nouns from Latin and Greek origin still retain their original plural form.	• *analysis, analyses; crisis, crises; thesis, theses* • *criterion, criteria; datum, data; phenomenon, phenomena; stimulus, stimuli*

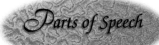

COUNTABLE AND UNCOUNTABLE NOUNS

Most nouns are countable.	• They have **five children**. • There are **twelve chairs** in this room.
Some abstract nouns are uncountable.	• **Freedom** is often taken for granted. • **Integrity** is necessary in business.
Many concrete nouns are uncountable.	• **Paper** is very expensive now. • **Water** is good on a hot day.

NOUNS AS MODIFIERS

When a noun precedes another noun, the first noun acts as an adjective and never takes an **-s** in the plural form.	• My friend bought some **opera tickets**. • I like the **shower curtains** with the **fish designs**.
When a combination of two nouns precede another noun, this combination is an adjective and it must be hyphenated. **These noun modifiers do not take the plural form.**	• This **seventy-five-year-old** man is my father. • My **nine-year-old** nephew will be going to a camp this summer.
Note: Some compound nouns are never hyphenated and make sense by themselves.	• The **birthday cards** he gets from his aunt are funny. • She loves **fine French cuisine**.

POSSESSIVE CASES

To show possession, use **-'s** at the end of singular and plural nouns (including those with irregular spelling) that do not already end in **-s**.	• I found **Nancy's shoes** under her bed. • These **children's parents** were sad to see them leave for school.
Use **-'s** to form the plural of numbers and letters.	• Mary's grades were good. She earned three **A's** and two **B's**. • Walk in **two's**, not **three's**.

If the possessor or "owner" is plural (ends in **-s** or **-es**), the apostrophe (') is added at the end.	• He read the **students' compositions**. • I don't know who the **horses' owner** is.
When the name of a person ends with an **-s**, add **-'s** or only an apostrophe (') at the end.	• **Charles's mother** got a raise. or • **Charles' mother** got a raise.
Add **-'s** to each name to indicate individual ownership, but only to the final name to indicate joint ownership.	• **Sam's and Jane's schools** were playing each other in basketball. (Sam and Jane go to different schools.) • **Sam and Jane's school** was playing in the tournament. (Sam and Jane go to the same school.)
An **-'s** is used with the indefinite pronouns **one, other, someone, somebody, nobody, anyone** to show possession.	• Here is **somebody's book**. • **Nobody's lesson** was ready.
A possessive noun appears without a following noun when the noun is understood.	• **Men's** problems are different from **women's** (problems). • The children are at the **dentist's** (office) today. • There is a sale at **Burton's** (store).
When speaking about things, we are more likely to use a phrase with **of**.	the colour **of the room**; the **sound of his voice**; the size **of the house**, etc.
However, it is common to use a possessive noun with: expressions of time, words related to natural phenomena, and words related to bodies or groups of people working together.	• **Time:** yesterday's storm, a week's visit, today's class • **Natural phenomena:** the sun's rays, the ocean's tides • **Bodies or groups:** the government's decision, the company's product, the city's water supply

Pronouns

Definition: A pronoun is a word used in place of a noun which refers to a noun or noun phrase. It acts as a noun in a sentence. Pronouns are grouped into the following categories:

PERSONAL PRONOUNS

Subject	I	you	he	she	it	we	you	they
Object	me	you	him	her	it	us	you	them

SUBJECT PRONOUNS

Subject pronouns replace the name of people or things and act as the subjects.	• **She** (Elizabeth) *has a terrific partner.* • **They** (the Italian students) *will leave for Rome in June.*

OBJECT PRONOUNS

Object pronouns replace the name of people or things and act as the direct or indirect objects of verb(s). A direct object answers the question **what?** or **who?** An indirect object answers the question **to whom? for whom? to what?** or **for what?**	• *He loves* **it** (direct object) *a lot.* • *Please read* **us** (indirect object) *the directions.*
Object pronouns act as objects to prepositions.	• *Give the book to* **him** (indirect object). • *Everyone looked at* **it** (indirect object) *carefully.*

POSSESSIVE PRONOUNS

Purely Possessive Pronouns	Possessive Pronouns-Adjectival
mine	my
yours	your
his	his
hers	her
—	its
ours	our
yours	your
theirs	their

Possessive pronouns show ownership by people. They can replace possessive adjectives and nouns.	• *This car is* **mine** (my car). • *His computer does not work, but* **hers** (her computer) *does.*
Possessive pronouns act as subjects or objects.	• *Their apartment is small, but* **ours** (subject) *is large.* • *Helen had good marks on her exams; however, Anne had weak ones on* **hers** (object).

Parts of Speech

REFLEXIVE PRONOUNS

Singular: myself, yourself, himself, herself, itself	
Plural: ourselves, yourselves, themselves	

Reflexive pronouns refer back to the subject(s) of the sentence. They are used when the subject and object are the same person.	• <u>I</u> often talk to **myself** when I'm alone.
Reflexive pronouns are used for *emphasis* when the object is the same as the subject of the sentence.	• <u>He</u> went **himself** to make sure everything was fine.
When reflexive pronouns are preceded with the preposition **by**, this expression means **alone**.	• She did it **by herself**. • I can do this **by myself**.

DEMONSTRATIVE PRONOUNS

Demonstrative pronouns replace known nouns. They are: **this, that, these,** and **those**.	• Do you see the <u>mountain of garbage</u>? I find **that** disgusting. • I've tried lots of different <u>chocolates</u> in my life, but **these** are the best! • **These** are my <u>socks</u>; **those** must be yours on the floor.

RELATIVE PRONOUNS

Relative pronouns join dependent clauses to a noun. They are: **who(ever), whom(ever), whose, which,** and **that**. Use **who, whom,** and **whose** for people. Use **that** and **which** for things. Note: See page 36 for additional information about using commas in relative clauses.	• The futon **that** I bought yesterday is uncomfortable. • I wonder if Bill Gates, **who** has more money than anyone else in the world, is a happy person. • "Ask not for **whom** the bell tolls . . ."

INTERROGATIVE PRONOUNS

Interrogative pronouns introduce questions. They are: **who(ever), whom(ever), whose, which(ever),** and **what(ever)**.	• There are two cars here. **Whose** will we take? • We have chocolate or white milk. **Which** do you prefer? • **What(ever)** do you mean by that?

IMPERSONAL AND INDEFINITE PRONOUNS

Impersonal/Indefinite pronouns refer to *nonspecific* persons or things.

Singular	Plural	Singular or Plural
another, anybody, anyone, anything, each, each one, either, everybody, everyone, everything, neither, no one, nobody, none, nothing, one, somebody, someone, something	both, few, many, most, much, others, several, such	all, any, some

IMPERSONAL

Use **one** instead of **you** when the subject is not known by the reader.	• **One** must try to achieve **one's** goals in life.

INDEFINITE

Use singular verbs with singular indefinite pronouns.	• There **is someone** at the door. • **Someone has** my car keys.
Use plural verbs with plural indefinite pronouns.	• **Several** of us **spend** money on books. • **Both** of them **are** gone for the weekend.
Indefinite pronouns **all, any,** and **some** can be followed by a singular or plural verb, depending on the antecedent.	• **All** (of the bread) **is** stale. • **All** (of the members) **are** present.

Adjectives

Definition: Adjectives modify nouns and pronouns, and they never take an -s in the plural form. They can be placed before the noun, after the verb *to be*, or after verbs that show state of being.

- *This **huge** house is very expensive. The **small** one is cheaper.*
- *Their **noisy** neighbours often get on my nerves.*
- *He is **tired**; she seems **rested**.*

POSSESSIVE ADJECTIVES

Possessive adjectives always precede nouns and never take an -s in the plural form. They modify subjects or objects (nouns).	• ***Their*** *dog barked during the night.* • *The artist lost **her** paint box.*
The possessive adjectives are: ***my, your, his, her, its, our, your, their.***	

DEMONSTRATIVE ADJECTIVES

These adjectives modify singular and plural nouns.

For *singular* nouns, use ***this*** and ***that***. **this** = refers to something (concrete or abstract) that is close to you, immediate or familiar in time or space **that** = refers to something that is far from you; not immediate in time or space	• ***This*** *coat is mine.* • ***That*** *afternoon was filled with surprises.*
For *plural* nouns, use ***these*** and ***those***. **these** = refers to things that are close to you, immediate or familiar **those** = refers to things that are far from you; not immediate	• ***These*** *are my ideas.* • ***Those*** *clouds look white and puffy.*

DEMONSTRATIVE ADJECTIVES *(continued)*

Note: With phrases like ***kind of, sort of and type of***, the demonstrative adjective modifies the noun ***kind, sort*** or ***type***, and must agree with it in number. Singular nouns: ***this/that*** kind, sort, type Plural nouns: ***these/those*** kinds, sorts, type**s**	• *I don't like **these sorts** of books.* • *What **kind** of question is **that**?* • ***Those types*** *of computers are affordable.*

ADJECTIVES OF COMPARISON

There are three degrees of comparison: equality, inferiority, and superiority.

COMPARATIVE DEGREE OF EQUALITY

To compare two things equally, use the adverb ***as*** before and after the adjective; the form of the adjective never changes.	• *The blue hat is **as** attractive **as** the brown one.* • *Montreal is **as** beautiful **as** Quebec City.*

COMPARATIVE DEGREE OF INFERIORITY

With adjectives of three or more syllables, use ***less*** and ***than*** to show comparative degree of inferiority.	• *Money is **less important than** good health.* • *Canada is **less populated than** China.*
For informal situations, the form: ***not as . . . as*** can be used.	• *It is **not as cold as** yesterday.* • *Often, people are **not as timid as** they appear.*

Parts of Speech

Parts of Speech

COMPARATIVE AND SUPERLATIVE DEGREE OF SUPERIORITY

	Positive	Comparative	Superlative
With adjectives of one or two syllables, add **-er** to the adjective followed by **than** for the comparative form, and add **-est** to the adjective for the superlative.	old	old**er than**	the old**est**
	fast	fast**er than**	the fast**est**
	clever	clever**er than**	the clever**est**
For one-syllable adjectives ending in a final single consonant preceded by a single vowel, double the final consonant and add **-er** and **than** for the comparative. Add **the** and **-est** for the superlative.	thin	thin**ner than**	the thin**nest**
	big	big**ger than**	the big**gest**
	hot	hot**ter than**	the hot**test**
For two-syllable adjectives ending with **-y** preceded by a consonant, change the **y** to **i** and add **-er** and **than** for the comparative, and use **the** and **-est** for the superlative.	easy	eas**ier than**	the eas**iest**
	funny	funn**ier than**	the funn**iest**
	tasty	tast**ier than**	the tast**iest**
For two-syllable adjectives ending in **-ous, -ish, -ful, -ing, -ed, -less, -ct, -nt, -st**, use **more** and **than** for the comparative, **the most** before the adjective for the superlative.	famous	**more** famous **than**	**the most** famous
	childish	**more** childish **than**	**the most** childish
	exact	**more** exact **than**	**the most** exact
For two-syllable adjectives ending in **-ow** and **-some**, add **-(e)r** or **more than** for the comparative, and use **-(e)st** or **the most** for the superlative.	narrow	narrow**er** or **more** narrow **than**	narrow**est** or **the most** narrow
	handsome	handsom**er** or **more** handsome **than**	handsom**est** or **the most** handsome

IRREGULAR COMPARATIVES AND SUPERLATIVES

Positive	Comparative	Superlative
good	better **than**	**the** best
bad	worse **than**	**the** worst
little	less **than**	**the** least
far (distance)	farther **than**	**the** farthest
far (additional)	further **than**	**the** furthest
old (age)	older **than**	**the** oldest
old (seniority)	elder **than**	**the** eldest

Adverbs

Definition: Adverbs modify verbs, adjectives, other adverbs, phrases and sentences. Some adverbs are formed by adding **-ly** to adjectives (*normal* → *normally*, *rapid* → *rapidly*).

- *He speaks **well**.*
- *This is a **very** stuffy room.*
- *They live in a **beautifully** renovated apartment.*
- ***Unfortunately**, it rained during our canoe trip.*

Note: To distinguish adverbs from adjectives, examine its function in a sentence.

- *The cityscape at night is **pretty**.*
  (Pretty is an adjective which modifies the noun "cityscape".)
- *You think you're **pretty** funny, don't you?*
  (Pretty is an adverb which modifies the adjective "funny", telling the reader how funny.)

There are hundreds of English adverbs that can be classified into the following groups:

ADVERBS OF AFFIRMATION/NEGATION

Affirmation: ***absolutely, certainly, obviously, surely, yes*** . . .	• *Nelson will **certainly** show up on time.* • *Chris is **obviously** lying.*
Negation: ***no, not, never, rarely***	• *I will **never** respond to that letter.* • *Bobby **rarely** visits his hometown.*

ADVERBS OF APPROXIMATION

almost, barely, exactly, nearly, practically, quite . . .	• *Are you **almost** finished?* • *We found the statement **quite** interesting.*

ADVERBS OF DEGREE/INTENSITY

completely, extremely, fairly, hardly, just, only, pretty, quite, rather, really, severely, scarcely, so, too, very . . .	• *That was a **fairly** intelligent comment to make.* • *You seem **rather** interested in linguistics.* • *It's **so** warm outside!*

ADVERBS OF FREQUENCY

always, continually, frequently, generally, occasionally, often, once, periodically, repeatedly, seldom, sometimes, usually . . .	• *I **always** back up my computer files.* • *George **repeatedly** comes to class late.*

ADVERBS OF INTERROGATION

when, where, why, how, how much . . .	• ***When** is the best time to talk?* • ***How** do you know when to sell stock shares?*

ADVERBS OF MANNER

abruptly, beautifully, briskly, carefully, eagerly, foolishly, graciously, happily, kindly, magnificently, reluctantly, thoughtfully, well . . .	• *This sculpture was **beautifully** crafted.* • *The offer was **graciously** declined.* • *Rolland speaks German **well**.*

ADVERBS OF PLACE

by, down, everywhere, far, here, near, nowhere, somewhere, there, up . . .	• *Why don't you swing **by** for a coffee?* • *How can you not see it? It's **everywhere** you look.* • *I don't live **far** from you at all.*

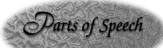
Parts of Speech

ADVERBS OF QUANTITY

almost, also, enough, many, most, much, several, too . . .	• I'm **most** willing to participate. • You seem **too** preoccupied to concentrate on the "here and now".

ADVERBS OF TIME

already, ever, just, now, soon, still, then, today, yet . . .	• I'm not hungry; I **just** ate. • Are you **still** waiting for a ride?

SENTENCE ADVERBS

These adverbs modify a complete sentence and usually express the writer's opinion.

actually, admittedly, apparently, certainly, clearly, definitely, fortunately, honestly, luckily, naturally, possibly, probably, surely, undoubtedly . . .	• **Actually**, the article was pretty enlightening. • We'll be there on time, **honestly**. • **Surely** someone will be able to explain all this.

ADVERBS OF COMPARISON

Comparative and superlative degrees of adverbs are formed in the same way as adjectives.

COMPARATIVE DEGREE OF EQUALITY

To compare two things equally, use **as** before and after the adverb; the form of the adverb never changes.	• She sings **as beautifully as** her sister. • They will come **as soon as** they can.

COMPARATIVE DEGREE OF INFERIORITY

To form the comparative degree of inferiority for adverbs, use **less** and **than**.	• He is older and drives **less carefully than** he used to.
For the superlative degree of superiority, use **the least** followed by the adverb.	• My house is **the least badly** renovated in the neighbourhood.

COMPARATIVE AND SUPERLATIVE DEGREE OF SUPERIORITY

	Positive	Comparative	Superlative
For one-syllable adverbs, add **-er** and **than** for the comparative and **the** with **-est** for the superlative.	hard	hard**er than**	the hard**est**
	swift	swift**er than**	the swift**est**
	soon	soon**er than**	the soon**est**
For adverbs with two or more syllables, use **more** and **than** for the comparative, and **the most** for the superlative.	vigorously	**more** vigorously **than**	**the most** vigorous
	quickly	**more** quickly **than**	**the most** quickly
	comfortably	**more** comfortably **than**	**the most** comfortably

Prepositions

Definition: Prepositions show the relationship of the object to the other elements of a sentence. Prepositions come before a noun or pronoun to create phrases that modify another word in the sentence.

PREPOSITIONS OF TIME

after, around/about, at, at the beginning of, at the end of, before, by, during, for, from/to, in, in the middle of, in time, on, on time, since, until (till)	• *The bank opens **at** 10:00 a.m.* • *It should be here **by** Monday.* • *The bus will arrive **in** 15 minutes.* • *Anne's birthday is **on** July 21.* • *They have not been to Paris **since** 1990.* • *There was an emergency and I left **in the middle of** the meeting.*

PREPOSITIONS OF PLACE OR POSITION

above, across, after, against, among, around, at*, at the bottom of, at the head of, at the top of, before, behind, below, beneath, beside, between, by, down, from, in*, in back of, in front of, inside, near, on*, on top of, outside, over, through, to, under, underneath, up	• *I'm going **to** the store.* • *My computer is placed **beside** my printer.* • *The closet is **beneath** the stairs.* • *There is an excellent cafe **down** the hill.* • *The memo he sent is **among** my papers.*
*Note: Use *at* when describing the location of things at a specific place, for a specific reason. Use *in* to express the location of things within a limited, three-dimensional context. Use *on* to express the location of things "resting on the surface" of a two-dimensional plane.	• *I was **at** the store when you called.* • *There's a hole **in** my favourite sweater.* • *Great. I have a spot **on** my jacket.*

PREPOSITIONS OF DIRECTION

by way of, into, out of, toward	• *We went **by way of** the tunnel that links France to Italy.* • *I walked **into** the room.* • *They ran **out of** the burning building.* • *He walked **toward** his parents.*

PREPOSITIONS OF MANNER

by, like, on, with	• *They go there **by** bus.* • *They went **on** foot.* • *We accept your invitation **with** pleasure.* • *He looks **like** his father.*

Parts of Speech

Conjunctions

Definition: A conjunction links words, clauses, or phrases. It shows the relationship between parts of a sentence. There are three categories of conjunctions: coordinating, correlative and subordinating.

Coordinating	Correlative	Subordinating
and, but, or, nor, for, so, yet	*both . . . and; either . . . or; neither . . . nor; not . . . but; not only . . . but also*	*after, although, as, as if, as though, because, before, even if, even, though, if, in order that, since, so that, than, that, though, unless, until, when, whenever, where, wherever, whether, while*

COORDINATING CONJUNCTIONS

Use a coordinating conjunction to unite words, phrases, and clauses of equal rank.	• *Drinking coffee keeps me awake,* **yet** *I drink it anyway.* • *We could go to the hockey game,* **but** *we decided to rent a movie instead.*

CORRELATIVE CONJUNCTIONS

Correlative conjunctions work in pairs to link words, phrases, clauses, or entire sentences.	• **Both** *of these students study hard* **and** *succeed.* • **Neither** *my roommate* **nor** *I will go to the baseball game.* • *I'll* **either** *rent a movie* **or** *go to the cinema.*

SUBORDINATING CONJUNCTIONS

Use a subordinating conjunction to join a subordinate clause (that cannot stand by itself) to a main clause.	• **When** *I was on my way to school, I saw one of my friends.* • **Although** *he is very tired, he will not rest.* • **Because** *I'm busy, I cannot go with you.* • **As** *he was speaking, I left the room.* • **Whenever** *he is in town, he calls on his friends.*

Articles

Definition: Articles are considered to be adjectives.

DEFINITE ARTICLE (THE)

The is used to modify a singular or plural noun that has been specified.	• *The apple in my hand was picked yesterday.* (a *particular* apple; not just *any* apple) • *Please give me the phone.* (a particular phone)
The is also used with technological and scientific terms.	• *The computer has replaced the typewriter.* • *The Giant Panda is in danger of extinction.*
Use **the** with an uncountable noun *only* when the noun describes a particularity.	• *____ Coffee is good in the morning.* • *The coffee in this can comes from Brazil.*
Use **the** before names of: *oceans, seas, groups of lakes, rivers, mountain ranges, points on the globe, geographic areas, deserts, forests, gulfs, archipelagos and peninsulas.*	*the Pacific Ocean, the Irish Sea, the Nile River, the Andes Mountains, the Equator, the Middle East, the Malay Archipelago, the Sahara Desert, the Gulf of Mexico . . .*
Do *not* use **the** before names of: *lakes and bays, a single mountain, continents, states, provinces, cities, *countries and streets.*	*__ Lake Ontario, __ Hudson Bay, __ Mount Everest, __ Australia, __ Montana, __ Alberta, __ San Francisco, __ Germany, __ Birch Street*

*Exceptions: *the United States, the United Arab Emirates, the People's Republic of China, etc.*

INDEFINITE ARTICLES (A, AN)

Indefinite articles *a* and *an* modify nouns that describe a generality.	• *I'm hot. Please open a window.* (any window)
Use *a* with words that begin with a *consonant sound.*	• *A mother often tells a bedtime story to a child.* (no specific mother, story or child)
Use *an* with words that begin with a *vowel sound.*	• *"An apple a day keeps the doctor away."* (any apple, any day)
*An is used before the word **honest** because the /h/ is silent. One hears the vowel sound [ɐ].	• **She is an honest woman.*

NO ARTICLE (Ø)

No article is used in front of indefinite plural nouns.	• *__ Cars are expensive these days.* • *Raising __ teenagers can be difficult at times.*
No article precedes the name of a state, province, city, country, street.	• *__ Paris is called the city of lights.* • *I was born in __ Vermont.* • *They live on __ Gage Street.*

Parts of Speech

Verbs

Verbs

Definition: Verbs express an action *(We **work** often.)*, condition *(His attitude **is getting** worse.)*, or state of being *(She **seems** tired.)*.

REGULAR VERB FORMS

Base Form	Infinitive Form	Present Participle	Past Participle
appear	to appear	appear**ing**	appear**ed**
listen	to listen	listen**ing**	listen**ed**
play	to play	play**ing**	play**ed**
smell	to smell	smell**ing**	smell**ed**
talk	to talk	talk**ing**	talk**ed**
taste	to taste	tast**ing**	tast**ed**
work	to work	work**ing**	work**ed**

TRANSITIVE AND INTRANSITIVE VERBS

Transitive verbs **require an object** or **indirect object**. Examples of transitive verbs: **buy, sell, make, put, discuss**	**Incorrect:** *Put the book.* **Correct:** *Put the book **on the table**.* (direct object = book; indirect object = the table) **Incorrect:** *Jana buys her mom.* **Correct:** *Jana buys her mom **lottery tickets**.* (direct object = lottery tickets; indirect object = her mom)
Intransitive verbs **do not require** an object. Examples of intransitive verbs: **read, walk, wait, fight, talk**	**Correct:** *Do you like to read books?* **Correct:** *Do you like to read?* **Correct:** *I become nervous when I talk to people I don't know.* **Correct:** *I become nervous when I talk.*

REGULAR VERB CONJUGATION (AFFIRMATIVE)

Example verbs: **to play** and **to work**

Simple Present Tense	1st person	I, you	work/play
	3rd person singular	he, she, it	work**s**/play**s***
	3rd person plural	we, you, they	work/play
Simple Past Tense (verb + ed)	1st person	I, you	worked/played
	3rd person singular	he, she, it	worked/played
	3rd person plural	we, you, they	worked/played
Future Tense (will + verb)	1st person	I, you	will work/will play
	3rd person singular	he, she, it	will work/will play
	3rd person plural	we, you, they	will work/will play

*The 3rd person singular takes an **-s** in present tense, unless an auxiliary verb is used.

Verbs

Auxiliary Verb Conjugation

The verb **to be** is used for all progressive verb tenses (present, past and future progressive).

Present	Past	Future	With Past Participle
I am	I was	I will be	I have been
you are	you were	you will be	you have been
he/she/it is	he/she/it was	he/she/it will be	he/she/it has been
we are	we were	we will be	we have been
they are	they were	they will be	they have been

The verb **to have** is used for all perfect tenses such as the present perfect, the present perfect progressive, the past perfect, the past perfect progressive, the future perfect, and the future perfect progressive.

Present	Past	Future	With Past Participle
I have	I had	I will have	I have had
you have	you had	you will have	you have had
he/she/it has	he/she/it had	he/she/it will have	he/she/it has had
we have	we had	we will have	we have had
they have	they had	they will have	they have had

The verb **to do** is used for all interrogative and negative forms of verbs in the simple present and simple past.

Present	Past	Future	With Past Participle
I do	I did	I will do	I have done
you do	you did	you will do	you have done
he/she/it does	he/she/it did	he/she/it will do	he/she/it has done
we do	we did	we will do	we have done
they do	they did	they will do	they have done

Normally, the third person singular takes an **-s** with all tenses, except with the auxiliaries **will** and **do/did**, which never take an **-s**.

Negative Forms

To form the negative, the basic formula is: present: **do not (don't) + main verb**	PRESENT • I *like* pizza. (affirmative) • I *do not like* pizza. (negative) *or* • I *don't like* pizza. (negative using contraction)
past: **did not (didn't) + base verb**	PAST • She *loved* that film. (affirmative) • She *did not love* that film. (negative) *or* • She *didn't love* that film. (negative using contraction)
future: **will not (won't) + base verb** **Note:** Avoid using the contracted form in formal writing.	FUTURE • They *will call* me tonight. (affirmative) • They *will not call* me tonight. (negative) *or* • They *won't call* me tonight. (negative using contraction)
With the verb **to be**, the negative forms are: present: **is not (isn't)/are not (aren't)** past: **was not (wasn't)/were not (weren't)** **Note: am not** cannot be contracted	• I *am not* young. • We *are not* sisters. • He *was not* in class last week. • You *were not* there yesterday.
Never use a negative modifier (*no, not, never*) with other negative words such as *no one, nothing, neither, none, nowhere,* etc.	**Incorrect:** There *isn't* ~~nothing~~ in the cupboard. **Correct:** There *isn't anything* in the cupboard.
Note: The words *any, anyone, anybody, anything, anywhere,* and *ever* are not negative.	**Incorrect:** She *doesn't* ~~never~~ go ~~nowhere~~. **Correct:** She *doesn't ever* go *anywhere*.

INTERROGATIVE FORMS

YES-NO QUESTIONS
These questions require an answer of either *yes* or *no*.

To form questions in the simple present, add *do* or *does*.	• *You have a car.* → *Do you have a car?* • *Andreas goes to college.* → *Does Andreas go to college?*
Use *did* to form questions in simple past.	• *Did they have fun yesterday?* • *Did I forget my keys again?*

QUESTIONS USING VERB "TO BE"

Invert the **subject** and the **verb** in any sentence.	• *He is my classmate.* → *Is he my classmate?* • *We are having fun!* → *Are we having fun?* • *She was funny.* → *Was she funny?* • *They were glad to see me.* → *Were they glad to see me?*

QUESTIONS USING AUXILIARIES

Invert the **first auxiliary** and **subject** in any sentence. Auxiliaries are: *to be*, *to have*, *to do*, and modals *(can, could, will, would, may, might*, etc.*)*	• *She can be there.* → *Can she be there?* • *I will have a lot of patience.* → *Will I have a lot of patience?* • *It makes sense.* → *Does it make sense?*

INFORMATION QUESTIONS
Question words are used when the subject of the question is unknown.

Question words include: *who, what, when, where, why, how, how much, how many, how often, how soon, how far*.	• *Who is coming to the party?* • *When will you be back home?* • *How far is your apartment from school?*

ACTIVE AND PASSIVE VOICE

Active verbs indicate that the subject of the sentence is the **"doer"** of the action.

Passive verbs indicate that the subject of the sentence is the **receiver** of the action. (The preposition "by" is often used or implied.) When the direct object is changed into a subject, the verb is in the passive voice. The subject of a verb in the passive voice does not act. A passive verb always consists of the verb *to be* followed by a past participle.

Verb Tenses	Active Voice	Passive Voice
Present	Mark **(subject and doer)** writes books.	Books **(subject and receiver)** are written by Mark.
Present Progressive	Mark is writing books.	A book is being written by Mark.
Present Perfect	Mark has written books.	Books have been written by Mark.
Past	Mark wrote books.	Books were written by Mark.
Past Progressive	Mark was writing books.	Books were being written by Mark.
Past Perfect	Mark had written books.	Books had been written by Mark.
Future	Mark will write books.	Books will be written by Mark.
Future Perfect	Mark will have written books.	Books will have been written by Mark.

Verbs

Verb Tense Overview

SIMPLE PRESENT (I *VERB*)

Function: Expresses action that is *general* or *permanent*.
Key words: generally, every day, frequently, often, always . . .

Conjugation	Negative Form	Question Form	Passive Form
	use **do not/don't** **does not/doesn't**	use **do** or **does** (don't modify the verb); invert subject and verb	**to be + past participle**
I usually **eat** at noon.	I usually **do not (don't) eat** at noon.	When **do I** usually **eat**?	Lunch **is eaten** at noon.
You/we (always) **like** it.	You/we **do not (don't) like** it.	How **do you/we like** it?	It **is** (always) **liked**.
He/she/it generally **works*** well.	He/she/it generally **does not (doesn't) work** well.	**Does he/she/it** generally **work** well?	
* 3ʳᵈ person singular takes **-s**		**Exception:** Don't use **do** with the verb **to be**. (e.g. Is she very talented?)	

PRESENT PROGRESSIVE (I AM *VERB*ING)

Function: Expresses a *temporary* action that is *in the present*.
Key words: right now, at this moment, now . . .

Conjugation	Negative Form	Question Form	Passive Form
to be + verb + -ing	add **not** after auxiliary	invert subject and auxiliary	**is being + past participle**
I **am reading** right now.	I **am not reading** right now.	**Are you** reading right now?	It **is being read** right now.
You/we **are waiting** for the bus (at this moment).	We **are not (aren't) waiting** for the bus.	Why **are we** waiting for the bus?	The bus **is being waited** for right now. The radio **is being listened** to.
He **is taking** swimming lessons.	He **is not (isn't) taking** swimming lessons.	**Is he** taking swimming lessons?	The swimming lessons **are being taken**.
Exception: verbs like *feel, hear, know, see, smell* and *want* do not normally take the progressive tense.			

Note: The progressive form is sometimes used to express future action. (i.e. I *am flying* to Europe. = I *will fly* to Europe.)

SIMPLE PAST (I *VERB*ED)

Function: Expresses an action that happened at a *specific moment in the past.*
Key words: yesterday, in 1967, one month ago, last Saturday . . .

Conjugation	Negative Form	Question Form	Passive Form
regular verb + **-ed**	use **did not/didn't**	use **did** (don't put **-ed** on verb); invert subject and auxiliary	**was/were + verb + -ed**
I **typed** the report last week.	I **did not (didn't) type** the report . . .	When **did I** type the report?	The report **was typed** . . .
David **registered** for the course last month.	David **did not (didn't) register** . . .	What **did David** register for?	David **was registered** . . .
You/We **studied** the texts two hours ago.	We **did not (didn't) study** . . .	**Didn't we** study?	The texts **were studied** . . .

Note: Irregular verbs take a special form in past tense. See page 30 for a list of common irregular verbs.

PAST PROGRESSIVE (I WAS *VERB*ING)

Function: Expresses an action that was *in progress at a specific moment in the past.*
Key words: during, when . . .

Conjugation	Negative Form	Question Form	Passive Form
was/were + verb + -ing	**was/were not + verb + -ing**	invert subject and auxiliary	**was/were + being + part participle**
I **was studying** when you called.	I **wasn't (was not) studying** . . .	What **was I** studying . . .?	It **was being studied**.
James **was talking** while I spoke.	James **was not (wasn't) talking** . . .	**Was James** talking . . .?	I **was being talked** to.
You/we **were cheering** during the football game.	You/we **were not (weren't) cheering** . . .	**Were we** cheering . . .?	The team **was being cheered** for.

PRESENT PERFECT (I HAVE *VERB*ED)

Function: Expresses an action that
  A) was experienced *sometime or repeated times in the past* **or**
  B) *started in the past and is not finished yet.*
Key words: since, for, never, ever, recently, yet . . .

Conjugation	Negative Form	Question Form	Passive Form
have + past participle	add **not** after auxiliary	invert subject and auxiliary	**has/have been + verb + -ed**
You/we **have visited** our parents several times.	You/we **have not (haven't) visited** . . .	How often **have you/we** visited . . .?	Our parents **have been visited** . . .
I **have played** hockey for two years.	I **have not (haven't) played** hockey . . .	How long **have I** played . . .?	Hockey **has been played** . . .
S/he **has** never **missed** a class before.	S/he **has not (hasn't)** ever **missed** . . .	**Has s/he** ever missed. . .?	A class **has** never **been missed** . . .

Note: **Irregular verbs** take a special form in present perfect tense. See page 30 for a list of common irregular verbs.

PRESENT PERFECT PROGRESSIVE (I HAVE BEEN *VERB*ING)

Function: Expresses action *started in the past and not finished yet.*
Key words: for five years now, recently, since (a specific time), lately . . .

Conjugation	Negative Form	Question Form	Passive Form
has/have been + verb + -ing	add **not** after first auxiliary	invert subject and first auxiliary	**N/A**
I **have been visiting** my mother often since she became ill.	I **have not (haven't) been** visiting . . .	How long **have I** been visiting . . .?	
He **has been playing** on the computer for hours.	He **has not (hasn't) been** playing . . .	**Has he** been playing . . .?	
You/we **have been counting** the days till your arrival.	You/we **have not (haven't) been** counting . . .	**Have you/we** been counting . . .?	

Past Perfect (I had *verb*ed)

Function: Expresses an action that happened *before another action at a specific moment in the past.*
Key words: until, before, when . . .

Conjugation	Negative Form	Question Form	Passive Form
had + verb + -ed	add **not** after auxiliary	invert subject and auxiliary	**had been + past participle**
I **had started** the work before it was due.	I **had not (hadn't) started** . . .	**Had I** started the work . . .?	The work **had been started** . . .
The class **had ended** before I arrived.	The class **had not (hadn't) ended** . . .	Why **had the class** ended . . .?	The class **had been ended** . . .
They **had used** typewriters until the computer was invented.	They **had not (hadn't) used** . . .	**Had they** used typewriters . . .?	Typewriters **had been used** . . .

Note: **Irregular verbs** take a special form in past perfect tense. See page 30 for a list of common irregular verbs.

Past Perfect Progressive (I had been *verb*ing)

Function: Expresses an action *in progress before a specific moment in the past.*
Key words: prior to, until, before, when . . .

Conjugation	Negative Form	Question Form	Passive Form
had been + verb + -ing	add **not** after first auxiliary	invert subject and first auxiliary	
I **had been smoking** for years until I became sick.	I **had not (hadn't) been smoking** for years . . .	**Had I** been smoking for years . . .?	N/A
She **had been playing** the drums for one hour when the neighbour finally complained.	She **had not (hadn't) been playing** . . .	What **had she** been playing . . .?	
Before the class, we **had been discussing** the homework.	Before the class, we **had not (hadn't) been discussing** . . .	When **had we** been discussing . . .?	

Verbs

FUTURE (I WILL *VERB*)

Function: Expresses a future action.

Key words: soon, tomorrow, next week/month/year, later on . . .

Conjugation	Negative Form	Question Form	Passive Form
will + verb; **am/is/are + going to**	add **not** after first auxiliary	invert subject and first auxiliary	**will be + verb + -ed;** **is going to be + verb + -ed**
I **will call** you next week. (I **am going to call** you . . .)	I **will not (won't) call** you . . . (I **am not going to call** you . . .)	**Will I** call you . . .? (**Am I** going to call you . . .?)	You **will be called** . . . (You **are going to be called** . . .)
He **will tow** the car tomorrow. (He **is going to tow** . . .)	He **will not (won't) tow** the car . . . (He **is not going to tow** . . .)	How **will he** tow the car . . .? (How **is he** going to tow . . .?)	The car **will be towed** . . . (The car **is going to be towed** . . .)
They **will change** their minds someday. (They **are going to change** . . .)	They **will not (won't) change** . . . (They **are not going to change** . . .)	When **will they** change . . .? (When **are they** going to change . . .?)	Their minds **will be changed** . . . (Their minds **are going to be** **changed** . . .)

Note: *Will* expresses **unpremeditated** future action. *Going to* suggests **premeditated** action.

FUTURE PROGRESSIVE (I WILL BE *VERB*ING)

Function: Expresses an action in progress at a *specific time in the future*.

Key words: when, tomorrow, tonight, next week/month/year . . .

Conjugation	Negative Form	Question Form	Passive Form
will be + verb + -ing; **is going to be + verb + -ing**	add **not** after first auxiliary	invert subject and first auxiliary	
I **will be working** on it when you are on vacation. (I **am going to be working** . . .)	I **will not be working** on it . . . (I **am not going to be working** . . .)	When **will I** be working on it? (When **am I** going to be working . . .?)	**N/A**
Anne **will be practising** the piano before the concert next week. (Anne **is going to be practising** . . .)	Anne **will not be practising** the piano . . . (Anne **is not going to be practising** . . .)	**Will Anne** be practising . . .? (**Is Anne** going to be practising . . .?)	
We **will be preparing** dinner tonight with our friends. (We **are going to be preparing** . . .)	We **will not be preparing** dinner . . . (We **are not going to be preparing** . . .)	**Will we** be preparing . . .? (**Are we** going to be preparing . . .?)	

FUTURE PERFECT (I WILL HAVE *VERB*ED)

Function: Expresses an action completed before a specific time in the future.

Key words: already, before, by (a certain time), when . . .

Conjugation	Negative Form	Question Form	Passive Form
will have + verb + -ed; **is going to have + verb + -ed**	add **not** after first auxiliary	invert subject and first auxiliary	**will have been + verb + -ed**
By the time you get here, **I will have** already **eaten** lunch. (. . . I **am going to have** already **eaten** . . .)	. . . I **will not (won't) have eaten** . . . (**I am not going to have** already **eaten** . . .)	Why **will I** have already eaten . . .? (**Am I** going to have already eaten . . .?)	Lunch **will have been eaten** . . . (The lunch **is going to have already been eaten** . . .)
Before tomorrow, you **will have opened** the letter. (. . . you **are going to have opened** . . .)	. . . you **will not (won't) have opened** . . . (. . . you **are not going to have opened** . . .)	When **will you** have opened . . .? (. . . **are you** going to have opened . . .?)	The letter **will have been opened** . . . (The letter **is going to have been opened** . . .)
They **will have paid** for the hotel room when we finally arrive. (They **are going to have paid** . . .)	They **will not have paid** . . . (They **are not going to have paid** . . .)	**Will they** have paid . . .? (**Are they** going to have paid . . . ?)	The hotel room **will have been paid** . . . (The hotel room **is going to have been paid** . . .)

Note: **Irregular verbs** take a special form in future perfect tense. See page 30 for a list of common irregular verbs.

FUTURE PERFECT PROGRESSIVE (I WILL HAVE BEEN *VERB*ING)

Function: Expresses an action that will be taking place up to a specific time in the future.

Key words: already, before, by (a certain time), when . . .

Conjugation	Negative Form	Question Form	Passive Form
will have been + verb + -ing	add **not** after first auxiliary	invert subject and first auxiliary	
By the year 2000, I **will have been teaching** for twenty years.	. . . I **will not have been teaching** . . .	. . . **will I** have been teaching . . .?	**N/A**
When you begin college, **we will have already been attending** school for five years.	. . . We **will not have already been attending** . . .	. . . **will we** have already been attending . . .?	
Before she plays in the concert, she **will have been practising** regularly for it.	. . . she **will not have been practising** . . .	. . . **will she** have been practising . . .?	

Verbs

Modal Auxiliaries

Modal auxiliaries are used together with main verbs to change the meaning or tone of a sentence.

Conjugation	Negative Form	Question Form	Passive Form	Special Information
• present = **modal + verb** • past = **modal + have + past participle**	**modal + not**	invert modal and subject	**modal + be + verb + -ed**	• Don't put **to** after a modal. • Use only **one modal** for one verb. • **Don't change the form** of a modal **according to person.**
• Suzanne **can fix** the lamp. • Suzanne **could have fixed** the lamp.	Suzanne **cannot (can't)** fix the lamp.	**Can Suzanne** fix the lamp?	The lamp **cannot be fixed** by Suzanne.	• I can ~~to~~ do it. • May I ~~can~~ do it? • She can~~s~~ do it.

Modal	Negative Form	Meaning(s)	Example(s)
can	cannot/can't	• ability, • possibility, • permission (informally)	• He **can** fly a plane. • Jane **can** go if she wants to. • **Can** I go with you?
could	could not/couldn't	• past ability, • possibility	• I **could** not lift it; it was too heavy. • He **could** be sick, but I'm not sure.
may	may not	• permission, • slight probability	• **May** I go home now? • I **may** see you tonight, I may not.
might	might not	• possibility (weaker possibility than "may")	• I **might not** eat dinner if I have a big lunch. • I **might** see you. (Don't count on it.)
must (have to/have got to)	must not/mustn't	• obligation, • strong probability	• You are ill and **must** (have to) see a doctor. • Her job **must** (has got to) be very difficult.
should (ought to)	should not/shouldn't	• suggestion, • advice	• You **should** (ought to) try the soup; it's great. • You **should** take care of the problem now.
will	will not/won't	• future intention	• I **will not** lie, even if the truth hurts.
would	would not/wouldn't	• polite request (would like), • past tense of *will*, • wish (would rather), • result of a condition	• I **would** like coffee, please. • He **wouldn't** help me decide. • I **would rather** not talk about this. • If I had more money, I **would** go to Europe.

Gerunds and Infinitives

Definition of a Gerund: Gerunds are nouns that end with an **-ing** form. Like nouns, gerunds can be used as the subject or object of a sentence.

- **Swimming** is a good exercise. (subject)
- I like **travelling**. (object)

An **-ing** form is a *present participle* when it is a *verb*.	• Our kids have fun **swimming** in the pool. • His parents enjoy **travelling** in Europe.
A gerund can be combined with a prepositional phrase.	• **Being in Europe** is an exciting experience for them. • **Travelling around the world** would be educational.
In formal writing and speaking, possessive adjectives and nouns sometimes precede the gerund in a gerund phrase.	• **Her dropping** out of school so suddenly surprised all her friends. • **His handling** of the situation was not acceptable to everyone.
Certain gerunds follow the verb *go* in idiomatic expressions.	• During the winter months we **go skiing**. • When I was a child, I used to **go fishing** with my dad.
Do not confuse a gerund with a progressive verb.	• Judith loves **hiking**. (gerund) • Judith **is hiking** right now. (present progressive verb)

GERUNDS AS OBJECTS OF CERTAIN VERBS

Some verbs cannot be followed by an infinitive.	**Incorrect:** I enjoy ~~to eat~~. **Correct:** I enjoy **eating**. **Incorrect:** I finished ~~to do~~ my homework. **Correct:** I finished **doing** my homework.
Some verbs that must be followed by a gerund are:	*admit, avoid, consider, deny, dislike, enjoy, finish, give up, keep on, miss, practice, put off, quit, recommend, risk, stop (quit), suggest, tolerate*
An *infinitive* follows the verb **stop** if it means to stop for a purpose.	• I **stopped to get** a loaf of bread at the store on my way home. • I **stopped to talk** to him for a while.
However, a *gerund* must follow **stop** when it means "to quit".	• He's finally **stopped** (quit) **smoking** after ten years.

RULES FOR VERBS "MAKE" AND "LET"

The verbs **make** *(to compel/force)* and **let** *(allow/permit)* are always followed by a(pro)noun plus a base form. The (pro)noun may be referred to as the **doer** that performs the action.	• The police **made the prisoner confess** her crime. • Please don't **let the rain come** in. • **Let me go**.
Never use an infinitive after **make** and **let**.	**Incorrect:** Please let me ~~to go~~ to the party. **Correct:** Please **let me go** to the party. **Incorrect:** Don't make me ~~to tell~~ a lie. **Correct:** Don't **make me tell** a lie.

Verbs

COMMON GO + GERUND CONSTRUCTIONS

Some common **go + gerund** constructions are:	go boating	go hiking	go sightseeing
	go running	go camping	go jogging
	go dancing	go shopping	go swimming
	Example: I go running every afternoon.		

COMMON PHRASAL VERBS FOLLOWED BY GERUNDS

Examples	Sentences
be anxious about	I'm **anxious about making** the presentation.
be excited about	He's **excited about joining** the club.
be hopeful about	I am **hopeful about finding** a new job.
be sorry for/about	I'm **sorry for leaving** you in such a bind.
forget about	**Forget about finding** your wallet; it's gone.
see about	We'll **see about increasing** your allowance.
speak about	We should **speak about renewing** the contract.
worry about	Mom **worries about having** her kids come home too late.
be responsible for	Ginnie **was responsible for leaving** the dog out in the rain.
forgive for	Please **forgive** me **for being** late.
make up for	How can I **make up for hurting** your feelings like that?
pay for	I'll **pay for sticking** my nose in their business.
prevent from	The fear of a ticket **prevents** me **from speeding**.

Examples	Sentences
be interested in	Who's **interested in listening** to your lies?
succeed in	Erin **succeeds in finding** jobs easily.
take pleasure in	He **takes pleasure in watching** others succeed.
approve of	I don't **approve of** you **wasting** time like that.
be (get) tired of	He's **tired of waiting** for your answer.
be afraid of	Max is **afraid of losing** his friend's trust.
be capable of	They seem **capable of handling** the job.
be fond of	We **are fond of discovering** new places.
be proud of	Fran is **proud of handling** the situation as she did.
get out of	Albert can't **get out of working** this weekend.
be intent on	I **am intent on graduating** this spring.
count on	You can **count on being** promoted this year.
depend/rely on	I can't **depend on having** you around.
insist on	George **insists on attending** school this fall.
keep on	Even when she knows she's wrong, she **keeps on arguing**.
plan on	I **plan on taking** my friends out for lunch.
be accustomed to	She's **accustomed to working** long hours.
be (get) used to	She's **getting used to taking** lower doses of medication.
look forward to	I **look forward to meeting** you.
object to	I **object to being** spoken to in that way.
get away with	You can't **get away with cheating** like that.

Non-Progressive Verbs

Certain verbs are *typically not* used in the progressive form. However, using certain non-progressive verbs in the progressive form denotes special meaning: **A)** a formal situation, **B)** a sense of progressive change/evolution in thought, **C)** deliberate use of the senses.
Examples:

A) The judges **will be hearing** the testimony. (formal court situation)

B) We **are hearing** a lot about you these days. (Speakers didn't hear about the person much before this time.)

C) I **am smelling** it. (deliberate use of smell)

Verbs that show *perceptions*		
Incorrect: I am hearing a bird. **Correct:** I hear a bird.		
feel	observe	smell
hear	perceive	taste
notice	see	

Verbs showing *intellectual states, emotions* and *attitudes*		
Incorrect: We are knowing each other. **Correct:** We know each other.		
adore	fear	presume
agree	feel (believe)	realise
appreciate	find	recall
assume	guess	recognise
believe	hate	recollect
care	hesitate	regret
consider	hope	remember
desire	imagine	respect
detest	know	see (understand)
disagree	like	suppose
disbelieve	loathe	suspect
dislike	love	think (believe)
doubt	mean	understand/wonder
envy	mind	value
estimate	need	want
expect	prefer	wish

Linking verbs that indicate *qualities* or *states of being*		
Incorrect: I am having a headache. **Correct:** I have a headache.		
appear	matter	belong
be	represent	contain
cost	resemble	have
equal	seem	own
weigh	signify	possess
look	sound	

Verbs

Common Irregular Verbs

Base Form	Simple Past	Past Participle
arise	arose	arisen
awake	awoke	awoken
be (am/is/are)	was/were	been
beat	beat	beaten
become	became	become
begin	began	begun
bend	bent	bent
bet	bet	bet
bite	bit	bitten
bleed	bled	bled
blow	blew	blown
break	broke	broken
bring	brought	brought
build	built	built
burn	burnt	burned/burnt
burst	burst	burst
buy	bought	bought
catch	caught	caught
choose	chose	chosen
cling	clung	clung
come	came	come
cost	cost	cost
creep	crept	crept

COMMON IRREGULAR VERBS *(continued)*

Base Form	Simple Past	Past Participle
cut	cut	cut
deal	dealt	dealt
dig	dug	dug
dive	dived/dove	dived
do	did	done
draw	drew	drawn
dream	dreamed/dreamt	dreamed/dreamt
drink	drank	drunk
drive	drove	driven
eat	ate	eaten
fall	fell	fallen
feed	fed	fed
feel	felt	felt
fight	fought	fought
find	found	found
fit	fit	fit
flee	fled	fled
fling	flung	flung
fly	flew	flown
forbid	forbade	forbidden
forget	forgot	forgotten
forgive	forgave	forgiven
freeze	froze	frozen
get	got	gotten

Base Form	Simple Past	Past Participle
give	gave	given
go	went	gone
grind	ground	ground
grow	grew	grown
hang	hung	hung
have	had	had
hear	heard	heard
hide	hid	hidden
hit	hit	hit
hold	held	held
hurt	hurt	hurt
keep	kept	kept
kneel	knelt	knelt
knit	knit/knitted	knit/knitted
know	knew	known
lay	laid	laid
lead	led	led
leap	leapt	leapt
leave	left	left
lend	lent	lent
let	let	let
lie (lie down)	lay	lain
light	lit/lighted	lit/lighted
lose	lost	lost

Base Form	Simple Past	Past Participle
make	made	made
mean	meant	meant
meet	met	met
pay	paid	paid
prove	proved	proven
put	put	put
quit	quit	quit
read	read	read
ride	rode	ridden
ring	rang	rung
rise	rose	risen
run	ran	run
say	said	said
see	saw	seen
seek	sought	sought
sell	sold	sold
send	sent	sent
set	set	set
sew	sewed	sewn
shake	shook	shaken
shave	shaved	shaved/shaven
shine	shone	shone
shoot	shot	shot
show	showed	shown

Verbs

Verbs

COMMON IRREGULAR VERBS *(continued)*

Base Form	Simple Past	Past Participle
shrink	shrank/shrunk	shrunk
shut	shut	shut
sing	sang	sung
sink	sank	sunk
sit	sat	sat
sleep	slept	slept
slide	slid	slid
speak	spoke	spoken
speed	sped	sped
spend	spent	spent
spill	spilled/spilt	spilled/spilt
split	split	split
spread	spread	spread
spring	sprang	sprung
stand	stood	stood
steal	stole	stolen
stick	stuck	stuck
sting	stung	stung
stink	stank/stunk	stunk
strike	struck	struck

COMMON IRREGULAR VERBS *(continued)*

Base Form	Simple Past	Past Participle
swear	swore	sworn
sweep	swept	swept
swim	swam	swum
take	took	taken
teach	taught	taught
tear	tore	torn
tell	told	told
think	thought	thought
throw	threw	thrown
understand	understood	understood
upset	upset	upset
wake	woke	woken
wear	wore	worn
weave	wove	woven
weep	wept	wept
win	won	won
wind	wound	wound
withdraw	withdrew	withdrawn
wring	wrung	wrung
write	wrote	written

Common Transitive Phrasal Verbs

Examples	Meanings	Sentences
ask over	invite	My nephew **asked** many of his friends **over** for a party.
bring about	cause to happen	Her discovery **brought about** conflicting ideas in science.
bring up	raise (children/ issues)	• They **brought up** five children. • I'm sorry to **bring** this **up**, but . . .
call off	cancel	The game was **called off**.
call up	telephone	He **called up** his mother when he arrived.
do over	do again	Claudia had to **do over** her assignment.
drop in on	visit unexpectedly	They **dropped in on** us while we were eating.
get in	enter (a car, taxi)	We **got in** his father's car.
get off	leave (a plane, train, bus, bike)	We **get off** the bus on Oak Street.
get on	enter (a plane, train, bus, bike)	They **get on** the plane at Dorval.
get out of	• leave (a car, taxi), • get a benefit from	• I **got out** of the taxi at Peel Street. • They **get** a lot **out** of this course.
get through with	finish	It's unpleasant, but let's **get through with** it.
go after	pursue	The police **went after** the thieves.
hand in	submit work to a teacher/boss	**Hand in** your assignments.
hand out	distribute	The teacher **handed out** the course plans.
hand over	submit	**Hand over** your paper; the exam period is over.
hold back	refrain	Can he **hold back** from telling a secret?
keep on	continue	**Keep on** doing good work!
keep up with	go as fast as	It's hard to **keep up with** him; he walks too fast.
lay off	end someone's employment	They were **laid off** last year.
leave out	omit	She was **left out** of the group.
let in	permit to enter	**Let** the dog **in** before you go to bed.
let off	allow to leave (bus, train, car)	The taxi **let** me **off** beside my home.

COMMON TRANSITIVE PHRASAL VERBS *(continued)*

Examples	Meanings	Sentences
look out for	be careful	**Look out for** the bears when you hike in the woods.
look over	examine	The doctor **looks over** her charts.
pass up	not use	Don't **pass up** this wonderful opportunity.
pick out	select	I want to **pick out** a nice gift for my sister.
pick up	• lift, • get	• **Pick** your clothes **up** off the floor. • The school bus **picks up** the kids every morning.
put back	return to its original place	The kids had to **put back** their toys.
put on	cover with clothes	**Put on** a hat; it's cold outside.
put up with	tolerate	I **put up with** her bad mood all day.
run into	meet accidentally	I hope we **run into** each other soon!
run out of	lacking some supply	We **ran out of** milk.
stay up	not go to bed	Don't **stay up** too late.
switch on	start a machine/ light	**Switch on** the lights; we cannot see.
take off	• remove clothing, • leave quickly	• **Take off** your sweater; it's too warm. • She **took off** without saying goodbye.
talk over	discuss	Let's **talk over** the problem.
tear down	destroy	The city will **tear down** the old building.
tear off	remove by tearing	**Tear off** the sticker on the window.
tear up	tear into small pieces	I **tore** the letter **up** and threw it out.
touch up	improve by making small changes	The document has mistakes and should be **touched up**.
try out	see if something works	**Try out** a car before buying it.
turn down	• reject, • lower the volume	• My proposal was **turned down**. • Please **turn down** the TV; it's way too loud.
turn in	submit	**Turn in** your reports as soon as possible.
turn on	start a machine	Would you **turn on** the TV, please?
use up	consume	They **used up** all the paper.

Verbs

Common Intransitive Phrasal Verbs

Examples	Meanings	Sentences
ask around	question many people	***Ask around*** for the answer.
back out	retreat	He got scared and ***backed out*** of the deal.
back up	• support, • go in reverse	• I'll ***back*** you ***up*** if you need it. • He ***backed*** the car ***up*** so she could get in.
break out	occur suddenly	He ***broke out*** in tears.
break up	bring an end to	We dated for several months, then ***broke up***.
catch on	become popular	Snowboarding is really ***catching on***.
catch up	overtake	He's walking too fast and I can't ***catch up***.
cheer up	make happy	You seem so sad right now. Try to ***cheer up***.
come off	become unattached	The stamp keeps ***coming off*** the letter!
come up	arise	Every time the topic ***comes up***, we argue.
drop out	quit	They ***dropped out*** of the race.
end up	get somewhere	I'm lost! How did I ***end up*** here?
get even	take revenge	People say "don't get mad, ***get even***", but I think that's mean.
fall behind	make slow progress	Don't ***fall behind*** in your work or you'll have problems later on!
get along	relate well	We ***get along*** well together.
get together	meet	We should ***get together*** tonight.
get up	rise from bed	I ***get up*** around 7 o'clock in the morning.
give up	quit	She finally ***gave up*** smoking.

COMMON INTRANSITIVE PHRASAL VERBS *(continued)*

Examples	Meanings	Sentences
go on	continue	***Go on*** with your conversation.
hang up	to replace the phone receiver on the hook	I got angry, so I ***hung up*** on her.
keep up	go as fast as	Slow down! I can't ***keep up***.
lie down	recline	I'm tired and need to ***lie down***.
look out	be careful	***Look out*** for the cars!
make up	reconcile	After fighting, we ***made up***.
pass out	faint	It was so hot that he ***passed out***.
run away	escape quickly	You can't ***run away*** from your problems; they'll always find you.
show up	appear	What time did he ***show up*** at the meeting?
shut up	be quiet (rude)	Don't tell me to ***shut up***!
sit down	take a seat	Would you like to ***sit down*** and talk about it?
stand up	rise	***Stand up*** so I can see how tall you are.
take off	depart (plane)	The plane never ***takes off*** on time.
throw up	vomit	It is common to ***throw up*** when you have the stomach flu.
wake up	awaken	What time do you ***wake up*** on weekends?
work out	• be resolved, • exercise	• We can ***work out*** any problem. • I ***work out*** at the gym twice a week.

Sentences

Phrase

Definition: A phrase has no subject and no verb; a phrase consists of a few words that make no sense by themselves.

Appositive Phrase – A noun (or noun equivalent) that precedes or follows another noun and identifies or explains it.	• John Glenn, **the first man in space**, made another space voyage at the age of 77.
Verbal Phrase – When a verb does not function as a verb in a sentence, it is verbal.	• **Wearing a hat** when you ski is a good idea.
Absolute Phrase – A noun (or noun equivalent) that modifies an entire clause or sentence.	• **My favourite shirt with all the holes in it** is hanging in the closet.
Prepositional Phrase – Consists of a preposition and its object (a noun or pronoun). Sometimes, the phrase is used as an adjective or adverb.	• Let's go **to the movies** tonight. • He ordered a hamburger **with mustard and relish**.

Basic Sentence

Definition: A sentence is composed of a subject, a verb, and an object or complement. It must also express a complete thought.
She (subject) *lives* (verb) *all alone in this huge **apartment*** (object).
Rolland (subject) *is* (verb) ***an engineer*** (complement).

Simple Sentence – Contains only one independent clause, but can have more than one subject or verb.	• **He sits** on the porch. • **Paul** and **Mark** share an apartment. • **Go** to the store and **buy** a loaf of bread. • **Karen** and **Anne went** home to **eat** dinner.
Compound Sentence – Contains two or more independent clauses joined by a semicolon or a coordinating conjunction.	• I came; I saw; I conquered. • I came, I saw, **and** I conquered.
Complex Sentence – Sentence composed of one independent clause and one or more dependent clauses.	• When I arrived home, I saw that the lights were still on. • While I was reading, the phone rang.

Clause

Clauses can be *independent* or *dependent*.

Independent Clause – An independent clause can stand by itself; it contains a subject, verb and object.	• **I write books.**
Dependent Clause – A dependent clause *cannot* stand by itself, although it contains a subject, verb and object. An independent clause is needed to complete it.	• **When he was doing his assignment,** he was interrupted by his friends.

TYPES OF CLAUSES

Adjective (Relative) Clause – A dependent clause that modifies a noun or pronoun. It's introduced by a relative pronoun *(who, whom, whose, that, which)*.	• People **who do not eat much and exercise a lot** are normally in good shape.
Note: Whose is the possessive form of **who**.	• People, **whose** native language is Spanish, often have difficulty pronouncing the [v] sound in English.
Use commas to set off **defining** relative clauses. The punctuated sentence carries a different meaning.	• My brother, **who likes to smoke**, is trying to quit. (I have only one brother, and he likes to smoke. The relative clause defines one characteristic of my brother.) • My brother who likes to smoke is trying to quit. (I have more than one brother, but I am referring to the one who likes to smoke.)

Adverbial Clauses – Express real or unreal conditions. These conditional statements consist of a conditional clause introduced by **"if"** followed by a result clause. "If" clauses can express the following:	
hypothetical *or* present unreal results **"if"** + **simple past verb** [if clause] **would** + **base form** [result clause]	• If I spoke English well, I would get a different job. (Hypothetical result: The person would change her/his job.) • If I had the time, I would go to the party. (Reality: The person has no time.)

past unreal results **"if"** + **past perfect verb** [if clause] **would** + **past perfect verb** [result clause]	• **If I had known** you were coming, **I'd have baked** a cake. (Reality: I didn't know you were coming.)
future possibility **"if"** + **present verb form** [if clause] **will** + **base form** [result clause]	• **If I have** the time tomorrow, **I will go** to the party. (Future possibility: S/he will go to the party.)
The verb **to be** has a subjunctive form in a present-unreal conditional clause. **Were** is used in all persons.	• **If I were** a millionaire, I would take it easy for the rest of my life. • **If she were** honest, her life would be easier.

Noun Clauses – Act as subjects, direct objects, indirect objects, or objects of prepositions in dependent clauses. They are introduced by the following: *that, what, who(ever), whom(ever), where, how, why, whether (not), whatever, whichever (one), wherever, however, if.*	• No one knows **where he lives**. • **To whom** is she writing? • **Whatever you want** is yours.
A noun clause can come from a statement that introduces a dependent clause beginning with **that**.	• Everyone knows **that we're going to move**.
If a noun clause begins with **that** and is considered as a direct object, **that** can be omitted. However, when following adjectives of emotion and feeling, the clause is adverbial and **that** can be used.	• She claims _____ she is the best student in the class. • They are proud **that** they graduated.

Punctuation

Never leave a space after the last word in a sentence and its mark of punctuation.

THE COMMA (,)

Commas help to clarify the meaning of sentences by separating or enclosing elements.

Use a comma in the following situations:

before **coordinating conjunctions** which join two or more independent clauses (*and, but, nor, for, so, yet*),	• He is normally *cheerful, but* today nothing is going his way.
between **adjectives** which modify nouns,	• Margaret Atwood earned her reputation as an *intelligent, talented* writer.
Note: Adjectives which precede compound nouns cannot be separated by commas, and the word order cannot be reversed.	• This is a *fine French restaurant*. • She is an *expert civil engineer*.
to set off **participle phrases** preceded by an independent clause,	• *When arguing,* people must still show respect.
to set off **adjective clauses** (extra information that is not essential to the meaning of the sentence).	• The CN Tower, *which is a famous tourist attraction in Toronto,* is an impressive structure.
Note: When the sentence contains essential information, no comma is needed.	• The man *wearing an old grey sweater* is my father. (Information about the sweater is necessary because it identifies which man.)

THE COMMA *(continued)*

to set off **appositive phrases**,	• The hump-backed dolphin, *a mammal living off the coasts of India, Pakistan and China*, is an endangered species.
to set off conjunctive adverbs (*moreover, however, nevertheless…*),	• They enjoy one another's company; *however,* they do not wish to live together.
to set off **modifying phrases** within a main clause,	• My mother, *as a matter of fact*, lost thousands of dollars in 1987.
to emphasize **contrast**,	• Dr. Jones is a general practitioner, *not a psychiatrist*.
after a **subordinate clause** that introduces a sentence,	• *When he arrived home,* he immediately put the concert tickets on the table.
to set off additional parts of **dates or addresses**.	• The meeting was held on *October 2, 1984, in Sherbrooke, Quebec,* Canada.
Note: If a date or address contains only one item of information, it is not set off from the rest of the sentence.	• The meeting was held on October 2 in Sherbrooke.
In a **direct quotation**, a comma must precede or follow a phrase.	• *"Thank you very much for your help",* he said.
Do not use a comma if only the month and year are given, or if the date appears as day-month-year.	• The war in the Pacific ended in August 1945. • 1 January 1999
A **person's name** can be set off by commas.	• If you don't like the way I do things, *Mark,* you can do them yourself.

Sentences

THE SEMICOLON (;)

The semicolon is used to join main clauses and separate phrases and clauses containing other punctuation.

If two main clauses are short and closely related, use a semicolon.	• *Please slow down; you're walking too fast.*
Two independent clauses joined by a conjunctive adverb should be separated by a semicolon or divided into two sentences.	• *He eats well and exercises regularly; consequently, he stays healthy.* • *He exercises regularly. Consequently, he stays healthy.*
Two independent clauses that are connected without a coordinating conjunction must take a semicolon.	• *I can't tell the twins apart; they look too much alike.*
Use a semicolon before a coordinating conjunction only if the sentence is long and contains a number of punctuation marks or contains complicated items in a series.	• *The weather forecast is depressing; tomorrow, rain; Tuesday, hail; Wednesday, more snow; and Thursday, an icy rain.*

THE COLON (:)

Use a colon at the end of a **complete sentence** to introduce a list, an explanation, or a long formal quotation (more than 4 lines).	• *In order to paint this room, I will need the following items: a ladder, a paint brush, some paint, and a few old cloths.* • *My favourite author wrote: "The effect of any writing on the public mind is mathematically measurable by its depth of thought. How much water does it draw? If it awakens you to think . . . then the effect is wide . . . ."*
Use a colon after a business letter salutation.	• *Dear Ms Jones:* • *Dear Sir/Madam:*
Use a colon between titles and subtitles.	• *Anne Frank: Diary of a Young Girl*

THE PARENTHESES ( )

Use parentheses to set off words, phrases, and whole sentences that add to the clearness and completeness of a sentence.	• *Queen Elizabeth I (1533-1603) had a remarkable personality.*
Use parentheses to set off figures and numbers marking items in a series.	• *The government should aid students by (1) giving more time to pay off tuition fees, (2) helping students get better jobs during the summer, (3) establishing more cooperative programs at the university.*

THE BRACKETS [ ]

Use brackets to set off phrases, figures or sentences.

Brackets can clarify, explain or correct the information in a direct quotation.	• *Emerson said, "In a virtuous action, I properly **am** . . . I add to the world." [Emphasis added.]* • *She [the mother] would not speak to the press.*

THE ELLIPSIS (. . .)

Use an ellipsis mark to indicate an omission of words in a quotation. Use four periods to indicate unfinished statements or the omission of the end of a statement.	• *Emerson wrote, "Belief and love . . . will relieve us of a vast load of care."* • *He said, "The play is an exciting melodrama . . . ."*

The Dash (–)

The dash is used to show a sudden change in thought or to separate certain *sentence* elements. When used sparingly, dashes are more effective than parentheses; they emphasize more the enclosed material. Use dashes to:

add emphasis to parenthetical information,	• Three prominent women–**Sister Theresa, Lady Diana, and Audrey Hepburn**–all helped people throughout the world.
set off parenthetical material only when commas are inadequate and misleading,	• These cities–**Paris, Vienna, and London**–are the most fascinating of all the cities we have seen up to now.
show a sharp break or turn in thought,	• "I can **explain**–at least, I hope I can".
set off a summary phrase or clause that follows a listing,	• Cream, butter, cheese, and ice cream–**these are the delicious foods that I cannot eat while I am on a diet.**
introduce a long list or explanation,	• **I can't believe how much she ate for lunch**–a steak, two large pieces of pie with whipped cream and a soft drink.
to replace vulgar/offensive words or parts of words,	• What the **h**– are you doing? • He's a **real** –!
suggest hesitant speech or an interruption in speech.	• I was–**er**–well, I was just trying to explain. • "Hey! Watch out for **the**–!" Just then, Peter was struck by the baseball.

The Hyphen (-)

Hyphens are *half as long as a dash* and are used to connect *word* elements. Use hyphens to:

spell out words or divide words into syllables,	• My name is spelled **J-a-i-m-e**. • **con-cen-tra-tion**
divide a word with more than one syllable at the end of a line (don't divide one-syllable words),	• There is no point in **questioning** my honesty.
to separate parts of a compound number,	• I turned **twenty-nine** last year. • She lives on Brock and **Forty-second** Street.
to make certain compound nouns,	• He's a **know-it-all**.
to combine words of a compound modifier (if it comes before the noun it modifies),	• She's a **high-profile** lawyer. • The medic gave him **mouth-to-mouth** resuscitation.
to combine certain prefixes with nouns/adjectives: **anti-, mid-, neo-, non-,** etc.	**anti-Drug Campaign; mid-autumn; neo-Nazi; non-conformist**

Sentences

QUOTATION MARKS ("")

Use quotation marks to repeat the exact words of a speaker or writer (to quote someone).	• *US President Kennedy said, "Ask not what your country can do for you, ask what you can do for your country".*
Do not use quotation marks in indirect quotation. (reported speech)	• *He said he would handle the Jackman's account himself.*
Use quotation marks to indicate the titles of newspaper columns, chapters of books, short stories, articles, essays, and poems, names of radio and TV episodes.	• *In class, we discussed one of Robert Frost's poems entitled "After Apple Picking".*
Use single quotation marks to enclose a quote within a quote.	• *Jana said, "The letter reads 'To whom it concerns', and I guess that's me."*

THE EXCLAMATION POINT (!)

Exclamation marks indicate strong emotion and should be used sparingly in formal writing.	• *Get out of here!* • *This is the nicest place I've ever seen!*

THE PERIOD (.)

End a sentence with a period.	• *Go to the corner and turn right.*
Use a period after some abbreviations.	*Mr., Ms., Dr., M.D., Ph.D.*
Most abbreviations composed of initial letters of names of organizations are written **without** periods.	*MIT, CBC, CBS, UCLA*

Capitalization

Capitalize the first letter of the following: names of weekdays and months, professional titles, cities, countries, languages, companies, streets, geographical locations, every word in a title except for articles and prepositions, first and last names of people.	*Sunday, January, Professor Jones, Boston, China, Chinese, Bombardier, Sunset Boulevard, the Rocky Mountains, The Catcher in the Rye, Céline Dion*

THE QUESTION MARK (?)

Question marks indicate a question or a doubt about information.	• *Why are you studying English?* • *My niece is five (?) years old.*

Direct vs. Indirect Speech

Definition: In *direct speech*, a speaker's words are written verbatim (word-for-word), and are set off with quotation marks. In *indirect (reported) speech*, the speaker's words are paraphrased or summarized and are not set off by quotation marks. When making the transformation from direct to indirect speech, the verb form changes. Usually, indirect speech is introduced with a past tense verb.

Direct Speech	Indirect Speech
Simple present "I work."	**Simple past** He reported that he worked.
Present continuous "I am working."	**Past continuous** He stated that he was working.
Simple past "I worked yesterday."	**Past perfect** or **simple past** He exclaimed that he had worked yesterday. He exclaimed that he worked yesterday.
Present perfect "I have worked."	**Past perfect** He mentioned that he had worked.
Past perfect "I had worked."	**Past perfect** He announced that he had worked.
Past continuous "I was working."	**Past perfect continuous** He claimed that he had been working.
Present perfect continuous "I have been working."	**Past perfect continuous** He admitted that he had been working.
Past perfect continuous "I had been working."	**Past perfect continuous** He said (that) he had been working.
Future "I will work."	**Conditional** He declared (that) he would work.
Future continuous "I will be working."	**Conditional Continuous** He proclaimed that he would be working.

Direct Speech with Modals	Indirect Speech with Modals
can "I can help you."	She said (that) she **could** help you.
could "I could help you."	She said (that) she **could** help you.
may "I may help you."	She said (that) she **might** help you.
might "I might help you."	She said (that) she **might** help you.
must "I must help you."	She said (that) she **must** help you.
should "I should help you."	She said (that) she **should** help you.
will "I will help you."	She said (that) she **would** help you.
would "I would help you."	She said (that) she **would** help you.

Sentences

Transitions

Definition: Transitions are words or phrases that link ideas.

TRANSITIONS TO ADD AN IDEA

again, also, and, and then, besides, equally important, finally, first, further, furthermore, in addition, in the first place, last, likewise, moreover, next, nor, second, third, too	• She got some help from her dad; **and then**, she continued building the loft by herself. • He has not shown up yet, **nor** will anyone else. • **First**, we got a speeding ticket, **then** we got a flat tire.

TRANSITIONS TO SHOW CAUSE AND EFFECT

accordingly, as a result, consequently, hence, so, then, therefore, thus	• We had no more vegetables at home; **therefore**, we went grocery shopping. • I wear glasses, **thus**, I am able to read. • I have too much work to do; **consequently**, I cannot go with them.

TRANSITIONS TO SHOW CONCESSION

certainly, even so, granted, of course, to be sure, with the exception of	• We're broke, **granted**, but we still need to pay the rent. • **With the exception of** a few students, most of them have succeeded. • **Even though** I love you, I'm not ready to marry you.

TRANSITIONS TO SHOW CONTRAST

but, however, in spite of, nevertheless, not withstanding, on the contrary, otherwise, still, yet	• He works hard; **yet** he can't pay his bills. • The weather is nasty; **nevertheless**, I'm going out for a walk. • Ride in the car with me now, **otherwise**, you'll have to take the subway.

TRANSITIONS TO SHOW EXAMPLE

for example, for instance, such as	• An apple does not contain, **for example**, as many calories as a cake. • It is a time **such as** this when I feel completely in control of the situation.

TRANSITIONS TO SHOW TIME

after a few days, afterward, at length, at the same time, currently, earlier, following, immediately, in the meantime, in time, lately, later, meanwhile, shortly, soon, subsequently, this time, until now	• **Earlier** this morning, they went swimming. • David will, **in time**, learn to tie his shoes. • The movie doesn't start until 6:00. What do you want to do **in the meantime**?

TRANSITIONS TO SHOW SUMMARY

finally, in brief, in conclusion, in short, to conclude, to summarise	• **In conclusion**, too many people seemed to be affected by this disease. • **In brief**, our vegetable garden was not a disappointment but a disaster. • **In short**, the economy is doing well and will continue to do so for some time.

Traps

Faulty Pronoun Reference

Faulty pronoun reference occurs when a pronoun does not clearly refer to or agree with its antecedent.

To make a statement clear and to avoid repetition, use pronouns instead of nouns.	• *The tree will lose ~~the tree's~~ **its** leaves in autumn.* • *Karen is an excellent writer. ~~Karen~~ **She** won an award last year.*
However, make sure that it is clear what the pronoun refers to. Sometimes, you must significantly revise a sentence to avoid an unclear (faulty) pronoun reference.	**Unclear:** *John told Paul that **he** is gaining weight.* (Who is gaining weight, John or Paul?) **Clear:** John said, "Paul, you're gaining weight." **Unclear:** *Anne told Karen that **she** did a good job.* (Who did a good job, Anne or Karen?) **Clear:** *Anne congratulated Karen and said that she did a good job.*

Be certain that each pronoun refers clearly to one word.	**Unclear:** *This college has many rules, but they do not obey all of them.* (What does **they** replace, *college, rules* or *students*?) **Clear:** *This college has many rules, but ~~they~~ **students** do not obey all of them.*
When the meaning of a sentence is obvious, there is no confusion with the pronoun.	**Clear:** *After the doctor gave George an injection, **he** cried for half an hour.* (Though **he** can refer to George or the doctor, George is obviously the one who cried.)
Do not use a pronoun to refer to a noun that is hidden (already used as a modifier).	**Unclear:** *When I stepped on its tail, it growled.* **Clear:** *When I stepped on its tail, the dog growled.*

Dangling Modifiers

Modifiers are words that give a certain quality to the word(s) they precede.

Definition: A dangling modifier usually comes at the beginning of a sentence, but does not relate to the main part of the sentence.

To fix a dangling modifier: 1) Make the subject appropriate to the sentence it applies to; *or*	**Incorrect:** *Visiting my nephew, the apartment was robbed.* **Correct:** *Visiting my nephew, I learned that the apartment was robbed.*
2) change it into a dependent clause.	**Incorrect:** *Hanging from the ceiling, I saw a spider.* **Correct:** *I saw a spider hanging from the ceiling.*

Traps

Misplaced Modifiers

Definition: A **misplaced modifier** is a single word located in the wrong place. Though some modifiers can be placed almost anywhere in a sentence without causing confusion, others require exact placement in a sentence.

Some modifiers can be placed almost anywhere in a sentence or clause without being misplaced.	• *The bus came down the hill **slowly**. **Slowly**, the bus came down the hill.* • ***Consequently**, they refused to vote. They, **consequently**, refused to vote.*
The following modifiers require exact placement in a sentence: ***almost, nearly, just, only, even, hardly, merely, scarcely***. The meaning of the sentence changes each time the modifier is moved.	• ***Only** he told me that he liked my sister. (Nobody else told me.)* • *He **only** told me that he liked my sister. (That is the only thing he did.)* • *He told **only** me that he liked my sister. (He did not tell anybody else.)* • *He told me **only** that he liked my sister. (He did not tell me anything else.)* • *He told me that **only** he liked my sister. (He thought everybody else disliked her.)* • *He told me that he liked **only** my sister. (He did not like anybody else.)* • *He told me that he liked my **only** sister. (I have no other sister.)*
An appropriate modifier comes immediately after the word(s) it is connected to.	**Incorrect:** *They talked while they were studying **in whispers**.* **Correct:** *They talked **in whispers** while they were studying.*

Faulty Parallelism

To achieve a sense of balance in writing, the words, phrases and clauses in a series should be similarly expressed (grammatically paralleled to one another).

Definition: Faulty parallelism occurs when items or ideas in a series are not similarly expressed.

Two words or groups of words joined by a coordinating conjunction must have the same grammatical form.	**Not parallel:** *The winters in Canada are cold and there is a lot of snow.* **Parallel:** *The winters in Canada are **cold** and **snowy**.* (Both are adjectives.) **Not parallel:** *He enjoys watching movies and he likes music.* **Parallel:** *He enjoys **watching** movies and **listening** to music.* (Both are gerunds.) **Not parallel:** *The apartment was bright with a lot of sun.* **Parallel:** *The apartment was **bright** and **sunny**.* (Both are adjectives.)
Comparisons using **than** or **as** must be logically and grammatically similar.	**Incorrect:** ***The cities** in Europe are older than North America.* **Correct:** ***The cities** in Europe are older than **the cities** in North America.*
The first half of a paired conjunction (**not only…but also; both…and; either…or; neither…nor**), must balance the second half.	**Incorrect:** *The new book is not only **longer**, but also **it is more difficult**.* **Correct:** *The new book is not only **longer** but also **more difficult**.*

Helpful Lists

COMMONLY MISSPELLED WORDS

absence	alleviate	characteristic
abundance	allotted	chief
academic	allotment	committee
acceptance	already	conceive
accessible	altar	conscience
accidentally	amateur	children
acclaim	annually	committee
accommodate	apartment	compatible
accompanied	apologetically	competition
accomplish	apologised	concede
accuracy	appearance	conceive
accurate	appropriate	conceivable
accustom	attendance	condemn
acquaintance	attitude	connotation
across	audience	conscience
actually	authority	conscientious
admittance	available	controlled
adolescence	beginning	convenience
advantageous	breath	correlate
advertisement	breathe	council
afraid	brilliance	counsellor
against	career	courteous
aggravate	carrier	deceive
aggressive	cemetery	department
all together	changeable	dependent

desirability	foreign	pronunciation
detriment	fortunately	relieve
development	forty	reminisce
dilemma	fourth	resources
disappoint	friend	roommate
dissatisfied	fulfil	satire
discussion	gaiety	schedule
disgusted	government	strength
dominant	guarantee	stretch
disillusioned	height	surrounding
dropped	hindrance	susceptible
efficiency	jealous	suspense
eighth	kindergarten	tendency
eligible	leisure	though
embarrassment	license	tragedy
endeavour	literature	truly
entrance	marriage	tyranny
environment	medicine	undoubtedly
equipped	mileage	vacuum
example	occurrence	vengeance
excellence	omit	warrant
exercise	opponent	weather
fallacy	parallel	Wednesday
familiar	practice (n.)	weird
February	practise (v.)	writing/written
fictitious	preferred	
finally	privilege	

Traps

Words That Sound the Same or Look Alike

Word	Part of Speech	Meaning
accept except	verb preposition	to receive willingly to exclude
advice advise	noun verb	words of counsel to warn or give instruction
affect effect	verb noun	to "act on" a result
are our	verb adjective	"to be" (plural) possessive case of "we"
bare bear	adjective noun	nude, without clothing the animal
breath breathe	noun verb	the air inhaled/exhaled in respiration to inhale and exhale air
cite site sight	verb noun noun	to identify a precise location vision
choose chose	verb verb	to decide/elect (present tense) to decide/elect (past tense)
cloths clothes	noun noun	fabrics garments for the body
desert dessert	noun noun	arid, sandy region something you eat
dinner diner	noun noun	evening meal restaurant
its it's	adjective subject/verb	possessive pronoun contraction of "it is"
know no	verb adverb	to understand or be familiar with opposite of "yes"

Words That Sound the Same or Look Alike *(continued)*

Word	Part of Speech	Meaning
hear here	verb adverb	to listen to something in or at this place
loose lose	adjective verb	opposite of "tight" to misplace
quite quiet	adverb adjective	"completely" or "entirely" silent/not loud
passed past	verb noun	to move beyond/past (past tense) a previous time
than then	conjunction adverb	used to show comparison "at that time"
their there they're	adjective adverb subject/verb	possessive case of "they" a specific location contraction of "they are"
threw through	verb preposition	past tense of "throw" in one side and out the other/"by means of"
to too two	preposition adverb noun	in the direction of "also" or "in addition" the number
were where we're	verb adverb subject/verb	past tense of "are" place contraction of "we are"
weather whether	noun conjunction	atmospheric conditions/temperature "if"
whose who's	pronoun pronoun	possessive case of "who" or "which" contraction of "who is" or "who has"
your you're	adjective subject/verb	possessive case of "you" contraction for "you are"

COMMON *FAUX AMIS*

COMMON *FAUX AMIS* *(continued)*

English	French	French	English
abuse	insulter, malmener	abuser	exploit, exaggerate, misuse
account	compte (rendu)	acompte	deposit, advance
actual	réel	actuel	present
actually	en fait, de fait	actuellement	now, at present
affair	aventure amoureuse	affaires	business
agenda	ordre du jour	agenda	agenda
alley	ruelle	allée	path
ancient	antique	ancien	old, former
assist	aider	assister (à un cours)	attend
attend	assister à; servir	attendre	wait
advertisement	annonce, publicité	avertissement	warning
balance	équilibre, reste, solde	balance	scales
benefit	avantage, profit	bénéfice	profit
bureau	service gouvernemental, commode	bureau	desk; office
cave	caverne	cave	basement
circulation	tirage (d'un journal)	circulation	traffic
command (n.)	maîtrise	commande	order
conductor	chef d'orchestre; chef de train	conducteur	driver
confidence	confiance	confidence	secret
cry	pleurer	crier	yell, shout
date	rendez-vous amoureux; datte	date	date

English	French	French	English
deceive	tromper	décevoir	disappoint
deception	tromperie	déception	disappointment
defend	soutenir; défendre	défendre (interdire)	forbid
delay	retard	délai	time (limit), deadline
demand (n.)	exigence	demande	request
demand (v.)	exiger	demander	ask
derange	rendre fou	déranger	bother
distraction	folie	distraction	entertainment
editor	rédacteur en chef, réviseur	éditeur	publisher
engagement	fiançailles	engager	hire
essay	dissertation, essai	essai	attempt, try
experience	expérience (de vie)	expérience (scientifique)	experiment
evidence	preuve, témoignage	évidence	obviousness
figure	silhouette	figure	face
fine (adj.)	raffiné, délicat, beau, etc.	fin (adj.)	thin, pointed, kind, etc.
fine (n.)	amende	fin (n.)	end
furniture	meubles	fournitures	supplies
gentle	doux	gentil	nice
hazard	péril, danger	hasard	chance
ignore	ne pas tenir compte de	ignorer	not to know; ignore
inconvenient	malcommode	inconvénient	drawback

Traps

COMMON *FAUX AMIS* (continued)

COMMON *FAUX AMIS* (continued)

English	French	French	English
infant	nouveau-né; bébé	enfant	child
injury	blessure	injure	abuse
inscription	inscription (sur un monument)	inscription	registration, enrolment; inscription
isolation	isolement, solitude	isolation	insulation
journal	revue spécialisée	journal	newspaper
journey	voyage	journée	day
language	langue; langage	langage	language
large	grand, vaste	large	wide, broad
lecture	conférence, cours magistral	lecture	reading
library	bibliothèque	librairie	bookstore
local	local (adj.)	local	room, office; extension
manifestation	démonstration	manifestation	demonstration, show
mechanic	mécanicien	mécanique	machinery
medicine	remède, médicament	médecin	doctor
novel	roman	nouvelle	news; short story
occasion	événement	occasion	opportunity
photograph	photographie	photographe	photographer
phrase	expression, locution	phrase	sentence
place	lieu	place	room, space
pleasant	agréable	plaisant	amusing
prejudice	préjugé	préjudice	wrong, damage

English	French	French	English
presently	bientôt	présentement	now
pretend	faire semblant	prétendre	claim, assert
professor	professeur	professeur	teacher; professor
quit	abandonner, cesser	quitter	leave
raisin	raisin sec	raisin	grape
relation	parent (autre que père, mère, frère, soeur)	relation	relationship; acquaintance
remark	faire une remarque	remarquer	notice
resign	démissionner	se résigner	accept, put up with
rest	se reposer	rester	stay
resume	reprendre, recommencer	résumer	summarize, sum up
reunion	retrouvailles	réunion	meeting
rude	impoli	rude	rough, hard, harsh
sensible	sensé, raisonnable	sensible	sensitive
severe	grave, âpre	sévère	stern, strict
souvenir	souvenir (objet)	souvenir	memory; recollection; memento
stage	phase, période; scène de théâtre	stage	practical training
store	magasin	store	window blind
student	élève	étudiant	(university) student
support	soutenir, entretenir	supporter	put up with
survey	passer en revue	surveiller	watch
sympathetic	compatissant	sympathique	nice, friendly